All My

PASSWORDS

Denise DeNicolo

Brock Haus Press
www.BrockHausPress.com

All My Passwords/Denise DeNicolo —1st ed.

ISBN-13: 978-1542671897
ISBN-10: 1542671892

TABLE of CONTENTS

A

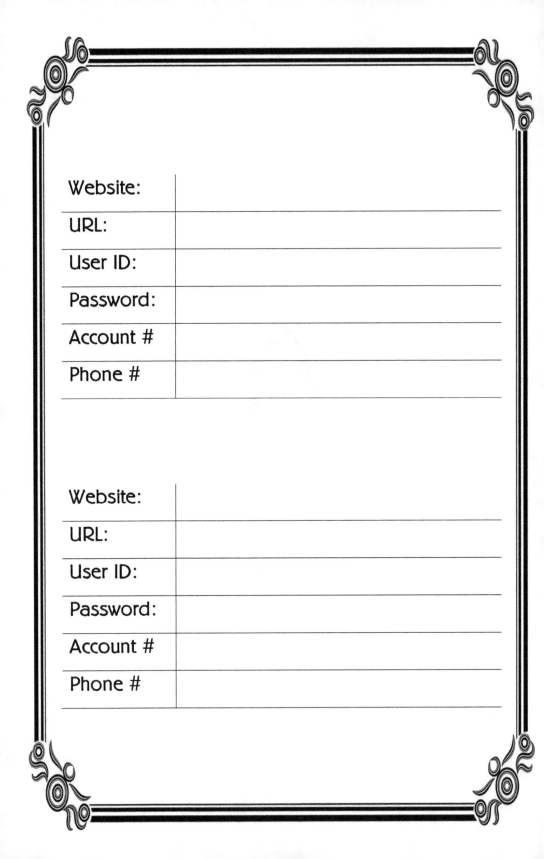

Website:	
URL:	
User ID:	
Password:	
Account #	
Phone #	

Website:	
URL:	
User ID:	
Password:	
Account #	
Phone #	

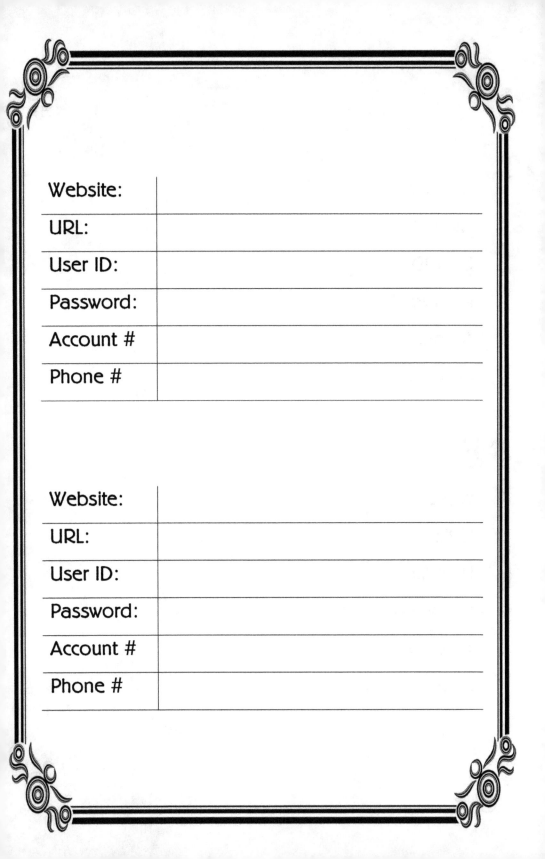

Website:	
URL:	
User ID:	
Password:	
Account #	
Phone #	

Website:	
URL:	
User ID:	
Password:	
Account #	
Phone #	

Website:	
URL:	
User ID:	
Password:	
Account #	
Phone #	

Website:	
URL:	
User ID:	
Password:	
Account #	
Phone #	

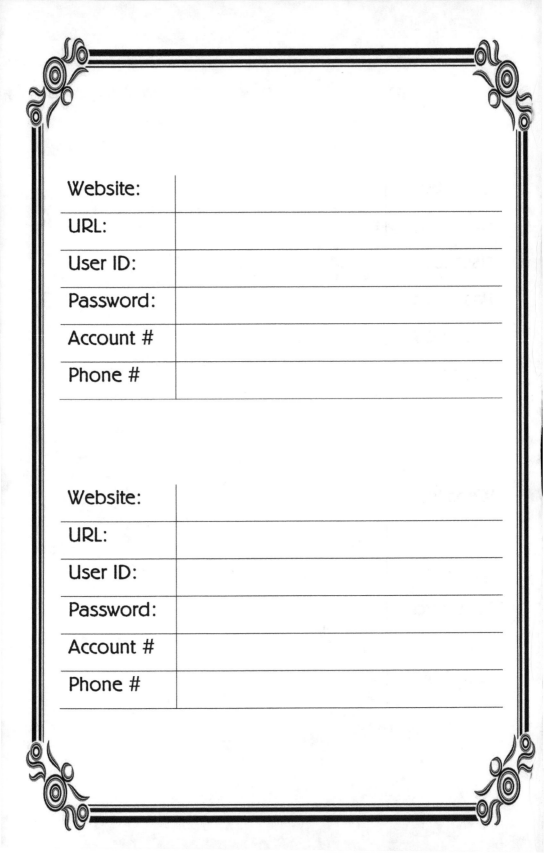

Website:	
URL:	
User ID:	
Password:	
Account #	
Phone #	

Website:	
URL:	
User ID:	
Password:	
Account #	
Phone #	

Website:	
URL:	
User ID:	
Password:	
Account #	
Phone #	

Website:	
URL:	
User ID:	
Password:	
Account #	
Phone #	

B

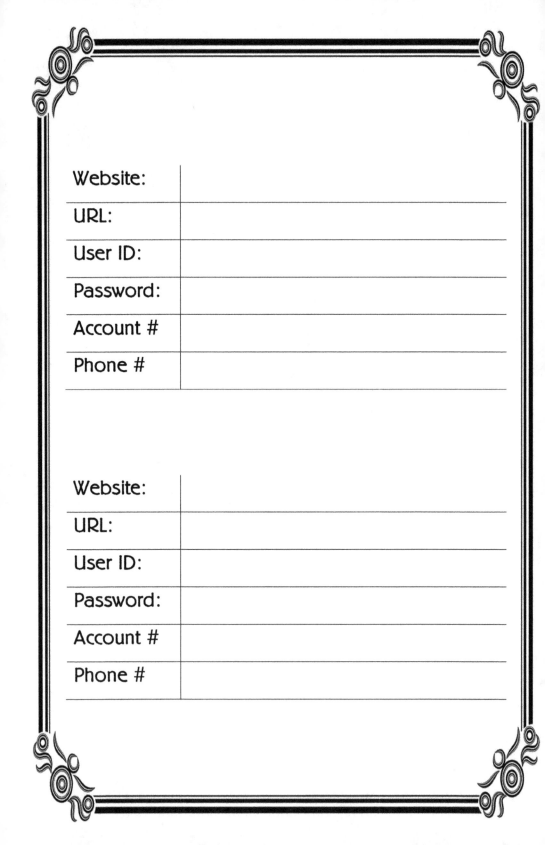

Website:	
URL:	
User ID:	
Password:	
Account #	
Phone #	

Website:	
URL:	
User ID:	
Password:	
Account #	
Phone #	

Website:	
URL:	
User ID:	
Password:	
Account #	
Phone #	

Website:	
URL:	
User ID:	
Password:	
Account #	
Phone #	

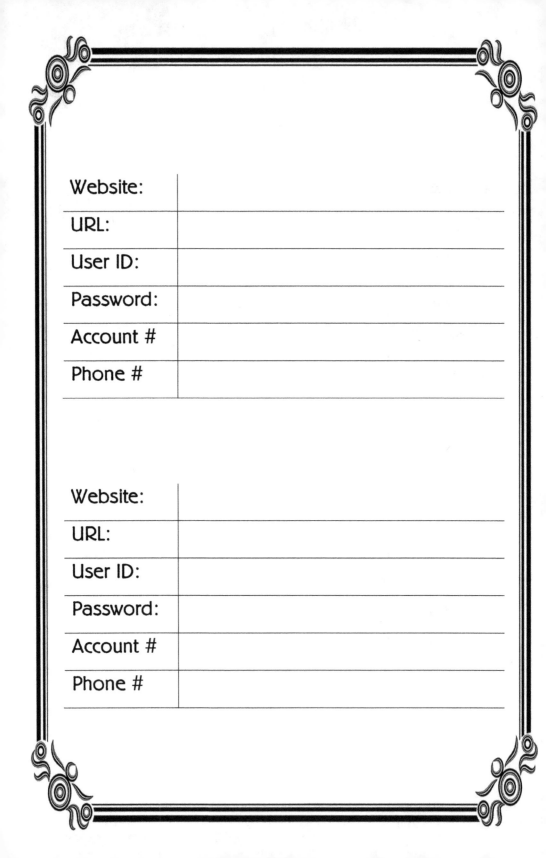

Website:	
URL:	
User ID:	
Password:	
Account #	
Phone #	

Website:	
URL:	
User ID:	
Password:	
Account #	
Phone #	

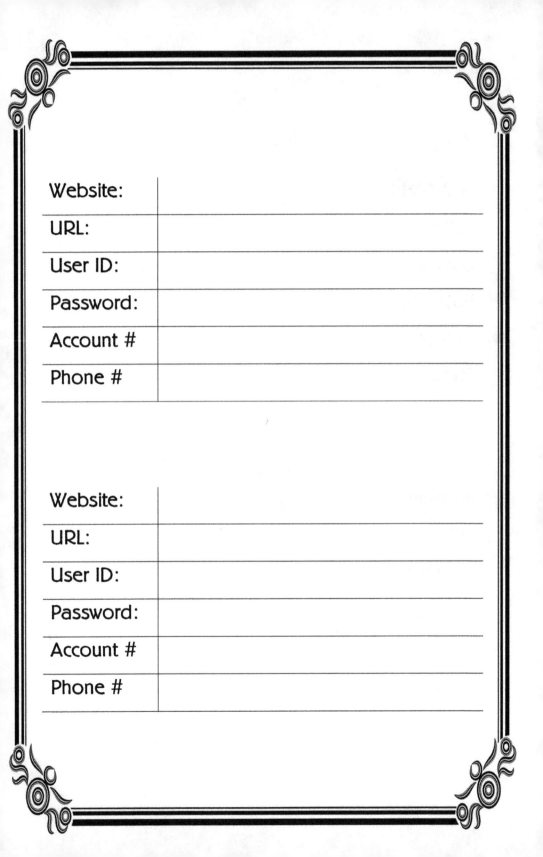

Website:	
URL:	
User ID:	
Password:	
Account #	
Phone #	

Website:	
URL:	
User ID:	
Password:	
Account #	
Phone #	

Website:	
URL:	
User ID:	
Password:	
Account #	
Phone #	

Website:	
URL:	
User ID:	
Password:	
Account #	
Phone #	

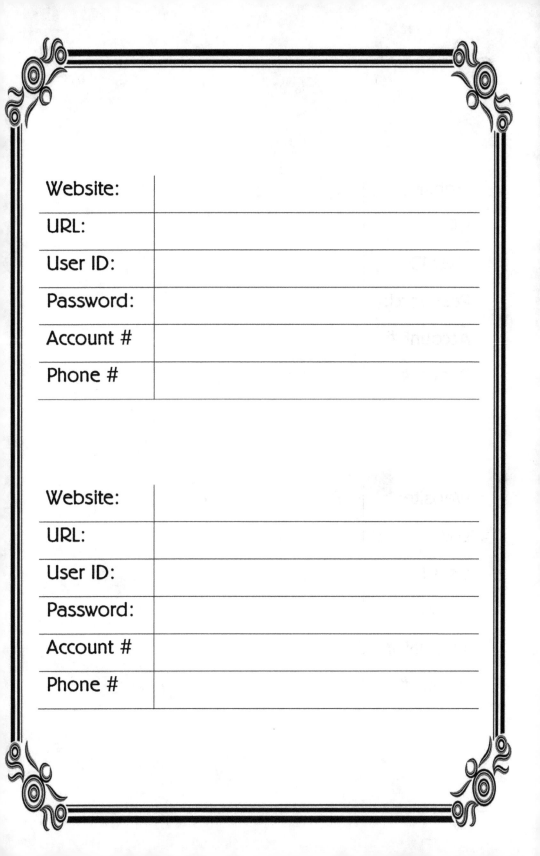

Website:	
URL:	
User ID:	
Password:	
Account #	
Phone #	

Website:	
URL:	
User ID:	
Password:	
Account #	
Phone #	

Website:	
URL:	
User ID:	
Password:	
Account #	
Phone #	

Website:	
URL:	
User ID:	
Password:	
Account #	
Phone #	

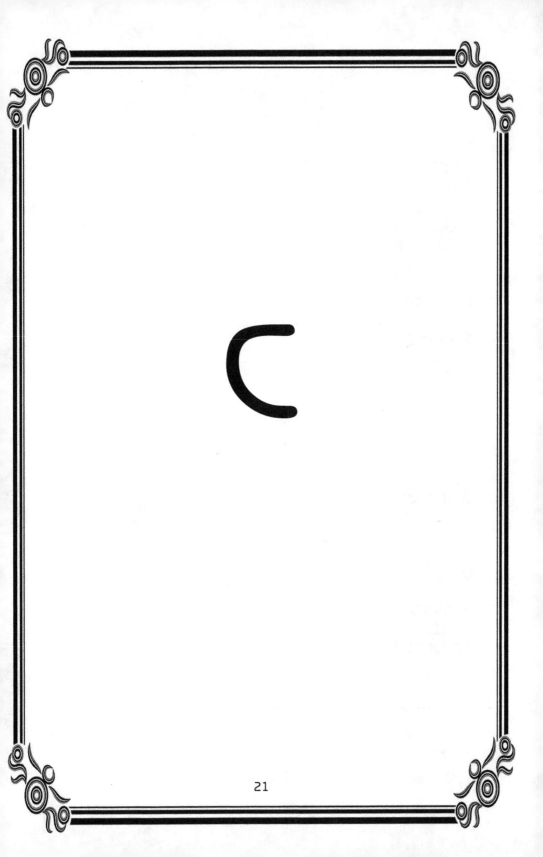

Website:	
URL:	
User ID:	
Password:	
Account #	
Phone #	

Website:	
URL:	
User ID:	
Password:	
Account #	
Phone #	

Website:	
URL:	
User ID:	
Password:	
Account #	
Phone #	

Website:	
URL:	
User ID:	
Password:	
Account #	
Phone #	

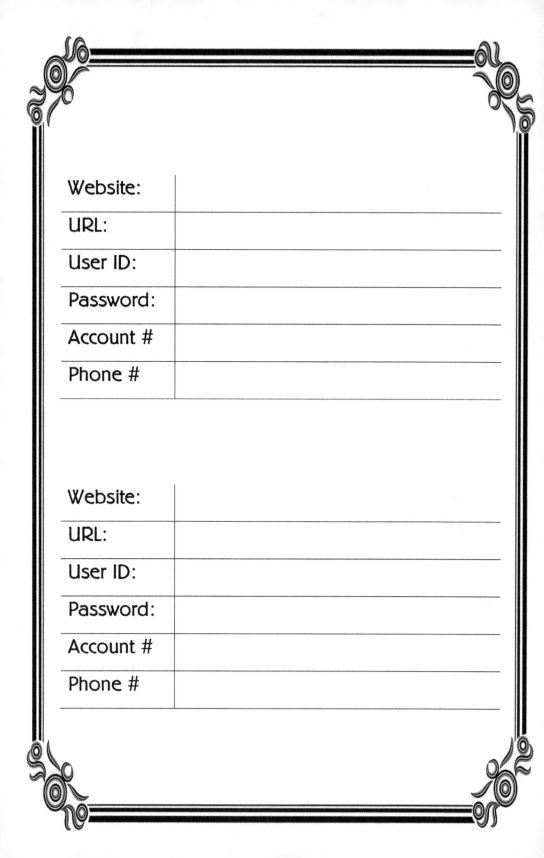

Website:	
URL:	
User ID:	
Password:	
Account #	
Phone #	

Website:	
URL:	
User ID:	
Password:	
Account #	
Phone #	

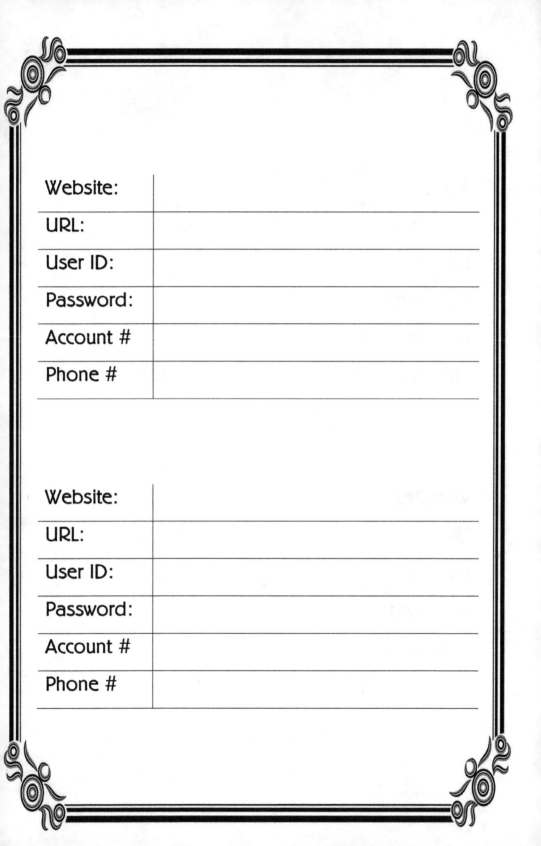

Website:	
URL:	
User ID:	
Password:	
Account #	
Phone #	

Website:	
URL:	
User ID:	
Password:	
Account #	
Phone #	

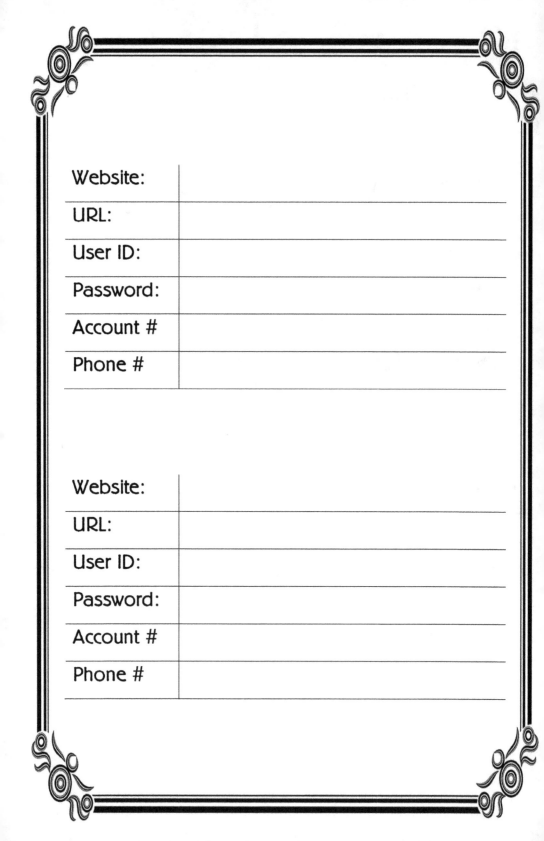

Website:	
URL:	
User ID:	
Password:	
Account #	
Phone #	

Website:	
URL:	
User ID:	
Password:	
Account #	
Phone #	

Website:	
URL:	
User ID:	
Password:	
Account #	
Phone #	

Website:	
URL:	
User ID:	
Password:	
Account #	
Phone #	

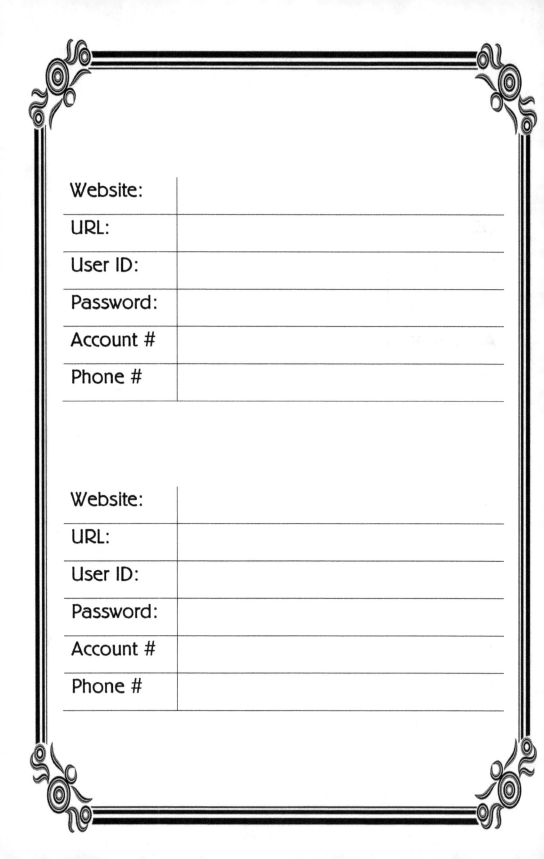

Website:	
URL:	
User ID:	
Password:	
Account #	
Phone #	

Website:	
URL:	
User ID:	
Password:	
Account #	
Phone #	

D

Website:	
URL:	
User ID:	
Password:	
Account #	
Phone #	

Website:	
URL:	
User ID:	
Password:	
Account #	
Phone #	

Website:	
URL:	
User ID:	
Password:	
Account #	
Phone #	

Website:	
URL:	
User ID:	
Password:	
Account #	
Phone #	

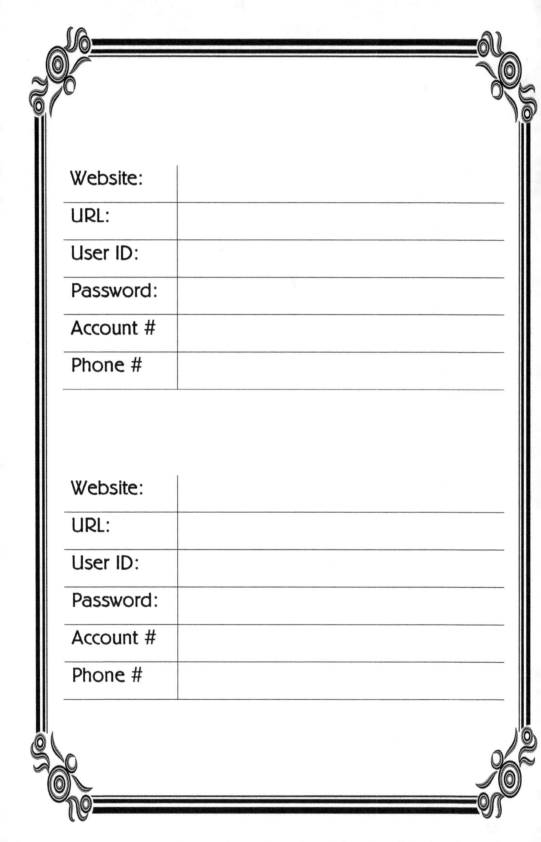

Website:	
URL:	
User ID:	
Password:	
Account #	
Phone #	

Website:	
URL:	
User ID:	
Password:	
Account #	
Phone #	

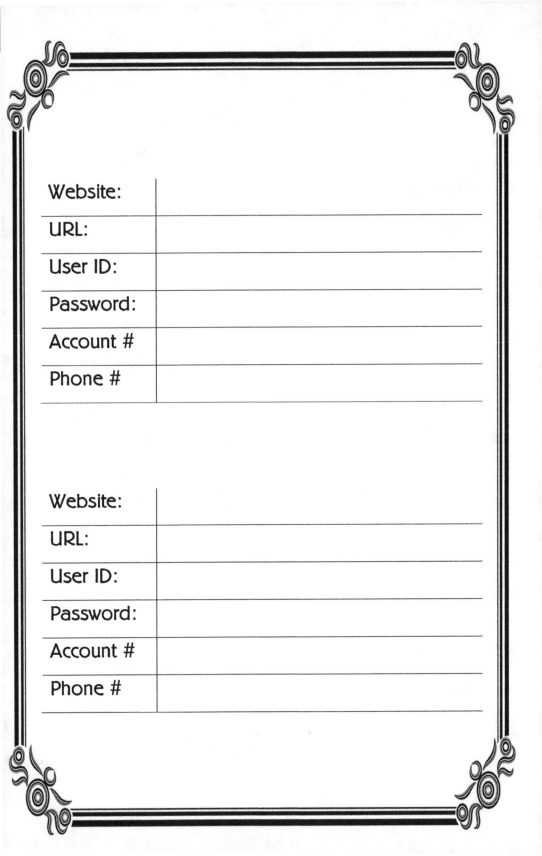

Website:	
URL:	
User ID:	
Password:	
Account #	
Phone #	

Website:	
URL:	
User ID:	
Password:	
Account #	
Phone #	

Website:	
URL:	
User ID:	
Password:	
Account #	
Phone #	

Website:	
URL:	
User ID:	
Password:	
Account #	
Phone #	

Website:	
URL:	
User ID:	
Password:	
Account #	
Phone #	

Website:	
URL:	
User ID:	
Password:	
Account #	
Phone #	

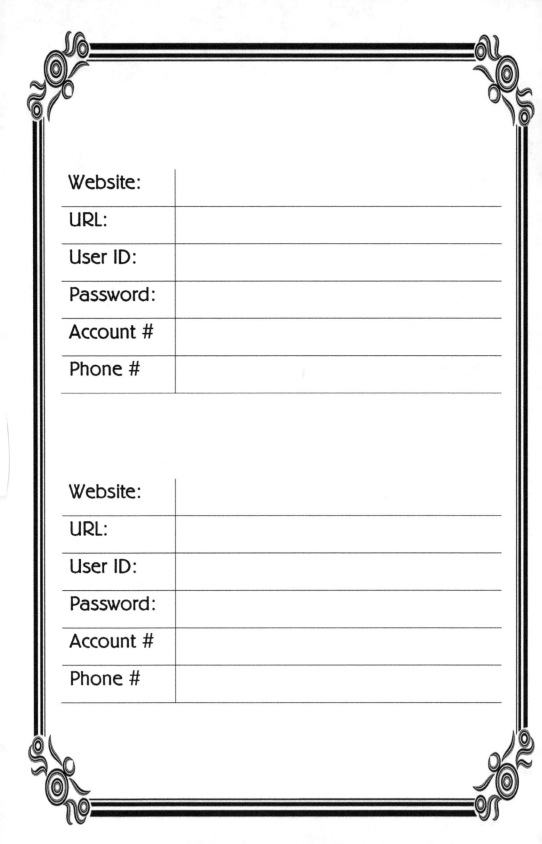

Website:	
URL:	
User ID:	
Password:	
Account #	
Phone #	

Website:	
URL:	
User ID:	
Password:	
Account #	
Phone #	

E

Website:	
URL:	
User ID:	
Password:	
Account #	
Phone #	

Website:	
URL:	
User ID:	
Password:	
Account #	
Phone #	

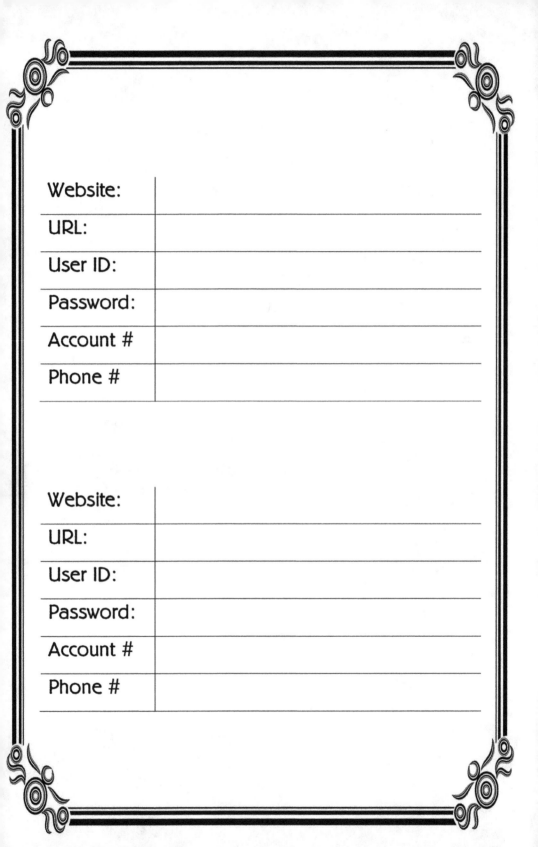

Website:	
URL:	
User ID:	
Password:	
Account #	
Phone #	

Website:	
URL:	
User ID:	
Password:	
Account #	
Phone #	

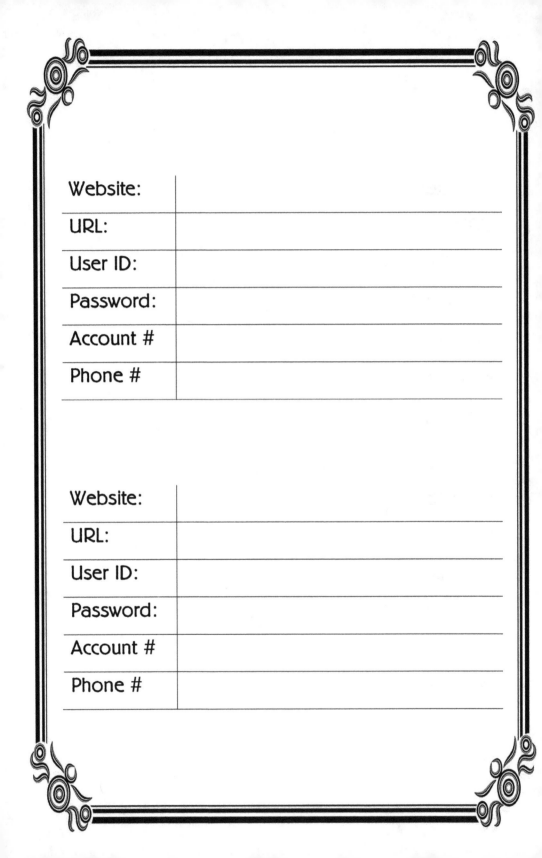

Website:	
URL:	
User ID:	
Password:	
Account #	
Phone #	

Website:	
URL:	
User ID:	
Password:	
Account #	
Phone #	

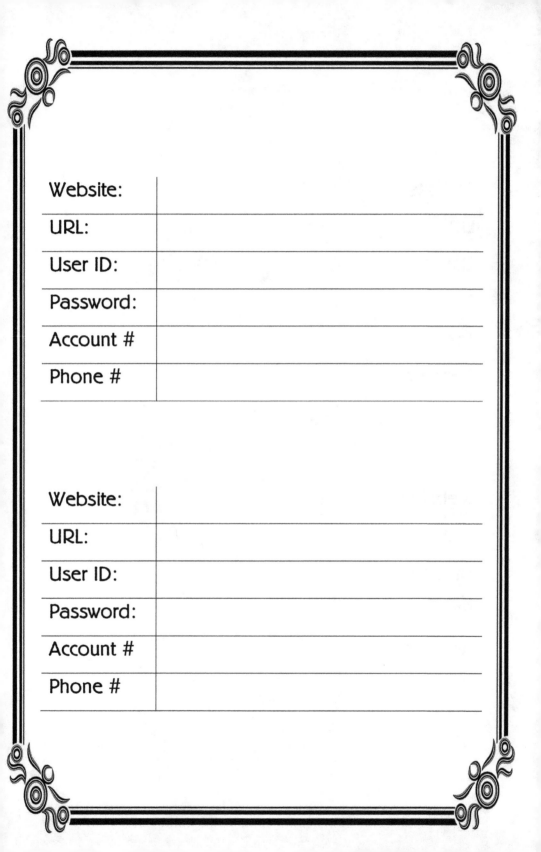

Website:	
URL:	
User ID:	
Password:	
Account #	
Phone #	

Website:	
URL:	
User ID:	
Password:	
Account #	
Phone #	

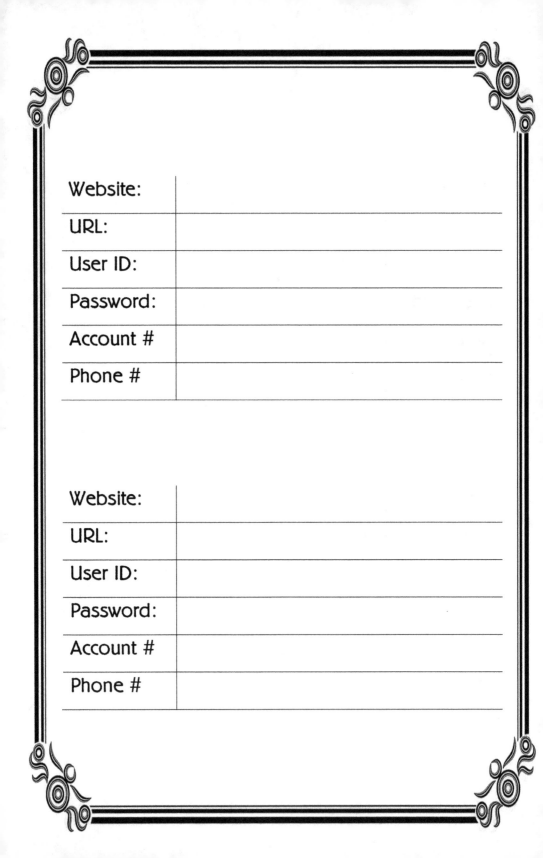

Website:	
URL:	
User ID:	
Password:	
Account #	
Phone #	

Website:	
URL:	
User ID:	
Password:	
Account #	
Phone #	

Website:	
URL:	
User ID:	
Password:	
Account #	
Phone #	

Website:	
URL:	
User ID:	
Password:	
Account #	
Phone #	

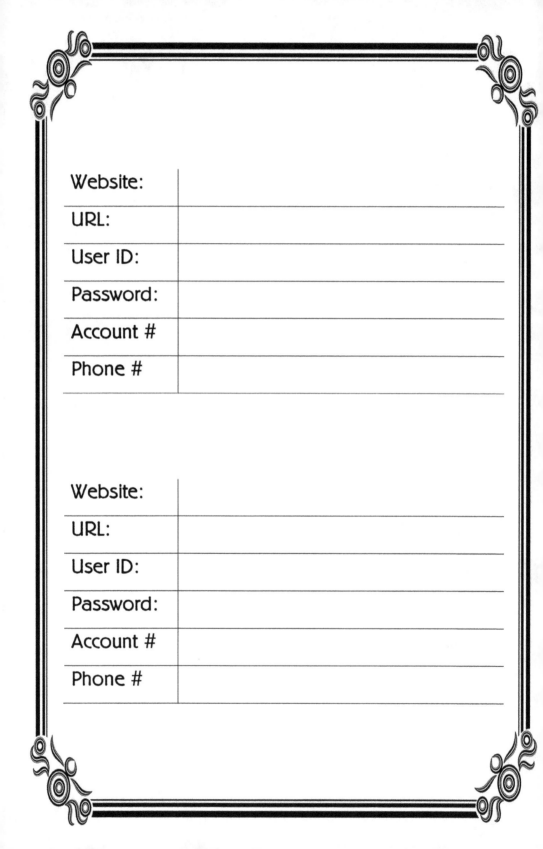

Website:	
URL:	
User ID:	
Password:	
Account #	
Phone #	

Website:	
URL:	
User ID:	
Password:	
Account #	
Phone #	

F

Website:	
URL:	
User ID:	
Password:	
Account #	
Phone #	

Website:	
URL:	
User ID:	
Password:	
Account #	
Phone #	

Website:	
URL:	
User ID:	
Password:	
Account #	
Phone #	

Website:	
URL:	
User ID:	
Password:	
Account #	
Phone #	

Website:	
URL:	
User ID:	
Password:	
Account #	
Phone #	

Website:	
URL:	
User ID:	
Password:	
Account #	
Phone #	

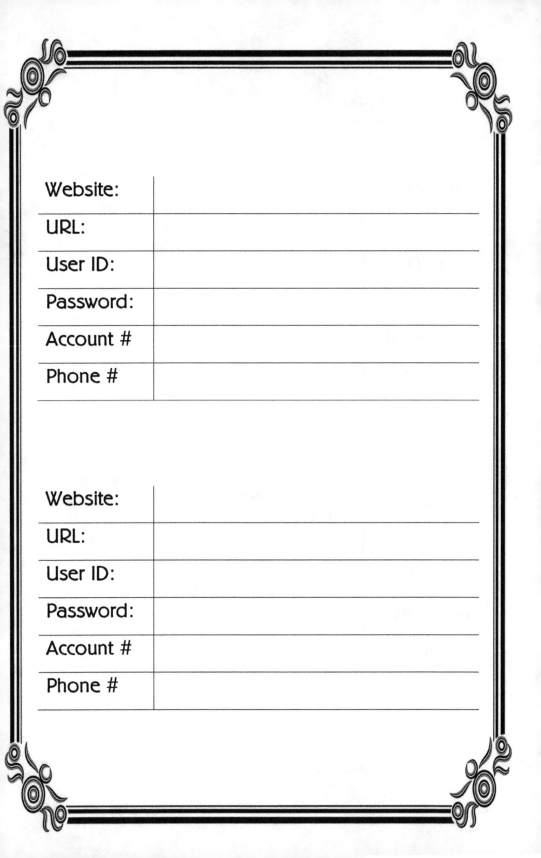

Website:	
URL:	
User ID:	
Password:	
Account #	
Phone #	

Website:	
URL:	
User ID:	
Password:	
Account #	
Phone #	

Website:	
URL:	
User ID:	
Password:	
Account #	
Phone #	

Website:	
URL:	
User ID:	
Password:	
Account #	
Phone #	

Website:	
URL:	
User ID:	
Password:	
Account #	
Phone #	

Website:	
URL:	
User ID:	
Password:	
Account #	
Phone #	

Website:	
URL:	
User ID:	
Password:	
Account #	
Phone #	

Website:	
URL:	
User ID:	
Password:	
Account #	
Phone #	

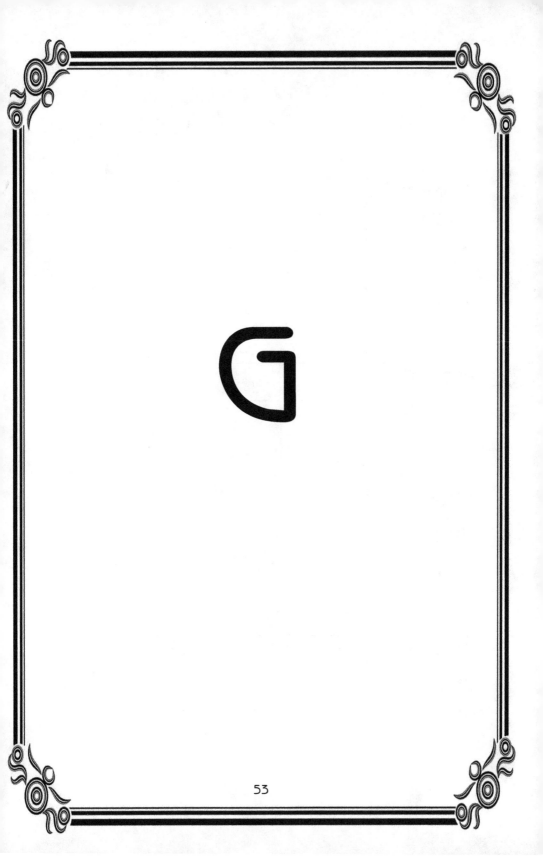

G

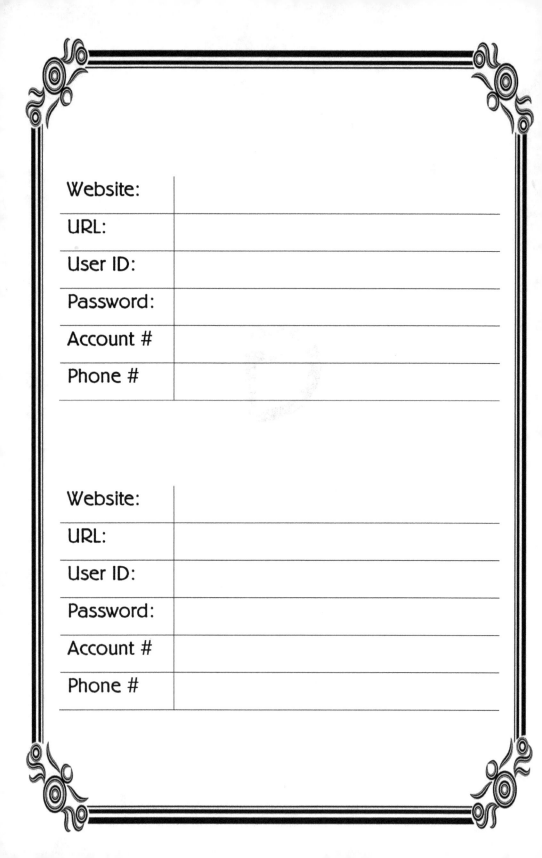

Website:	
URL:	
User ID:	
Password:	
Account #	
Phone #	

Website:	
URL:	
User ID:	
Password:	
Account #	
Phone #	

Website:	
URL:	
User ID:	
Password:	
Account #	
Phone #	

Website:	
URL:	
User ID:	
Password:	
Account #	
Phone #	

Website:	
URL:	
User ID:	
Password:	
Account #	
Phone #	

Website:	
URL:	
User ID:	
Password:	
Account #	
Phone #	

Website:	
URL:	
User ID:	
Password:	
Account #	
Phone #	

Website:	
URL:	
User ID:	
Password:	
Account #	
Phone #	

Website:	
URL:	
User ID:	
Password:	
Account #	
Phone #	

Website:	
URL:	
User ID:	
Password:	
Account #	
Phone #	

Website:	
URL:	
User ID:	
Password:	
Account #	
Phone #	

Website:	
URL:	
User ID:	
Password:	
Account #	
Phone #	

Website:	
URL:	
User ID:	
Password:	
Account #	
Phone #	

Website:	
URL:	
User ID:	
Password:	
Account #	
Phone #	

H

Website:	
URL:	
User ID:	
Password:	
Account #	
Phone #	

Website:	
URL:	
User ID:	
Password:	
Account #	
Phone #	

Website:	
URL:	
User ID:	
Password:	
Account #	
Phone #	

Website:	
URL:	
User ID:	
Password:	
Account #	
Phone #	

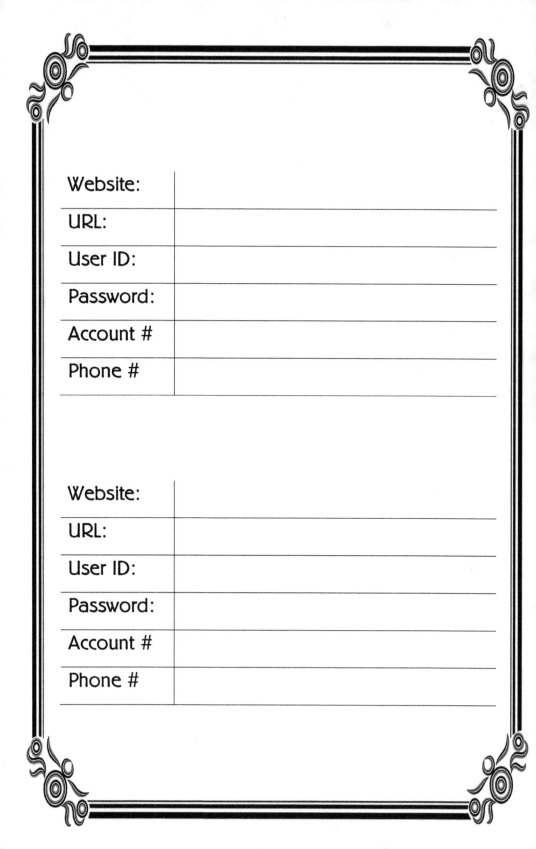

Website:	
URL:	
User ID:	
Password:	
Account #	
Phone #	

Website:	
URL:	
User ID:	
Password:	
Account #	
Phone #	

Website:	
URL:	
User ID:	
Password:	
Account #	
Phone #	

Website:	
URL:	
User ID:	
Password:	
Account #	
Phone #	

Website:	
URL:	
User ID:	
Password:	
Account #	
Phone #	

Website:	
URL:	
User ID:	
Password:	
Account #	
Phone #	

Website:	
URL:	
User ID:	
Password:	
Account #	
Phone #	

Website:	
URL:	
User ID:	
Password:	
Account #	
Phone #	

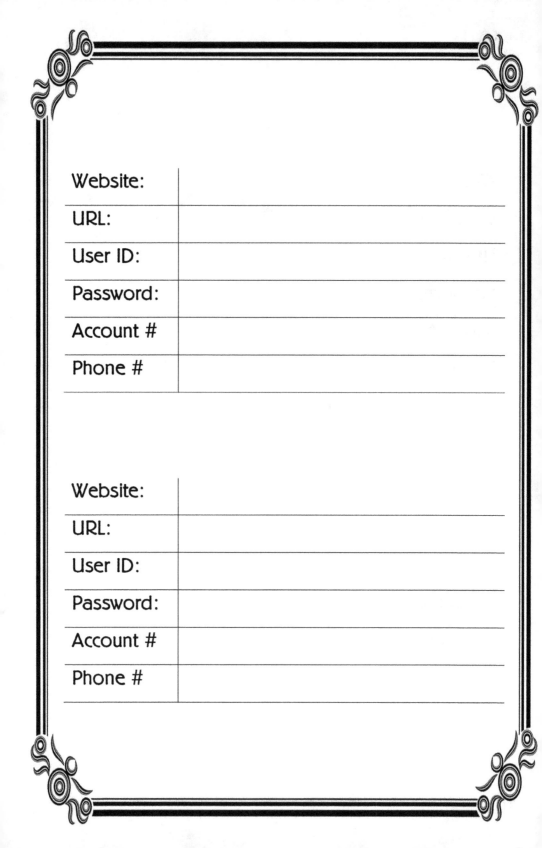

Website:	
URL:	
User ID:	
Password:	
Account #	
Phone #	

Website:	
URL:	
User ID:	
Password:	
Account #	
Phone #	

Website:	
URL:	
User ID:	
Password:	
Account #	
Phone #	

Website:	
URL:	
User ID:	
Password:	
Account #	
Phone #	

Website:	
URL:	
User ID:	
Password:	
Account #	
Phone #	

Website:	
URL:	
User ID:	
Password:	
Account #	
Phone #	

Website:	
URL:	
User ID:	
Password:	
Account #	
Phone #	

Website:	
URL:	
User ID:	
Password:	
Account #	
Phone #	

Website:	
URL:	
User ID:	
Password:	
Account #	
Phone #	

Website:	
URL:	
User ID:	
Password:	
Account #	
Phone #	

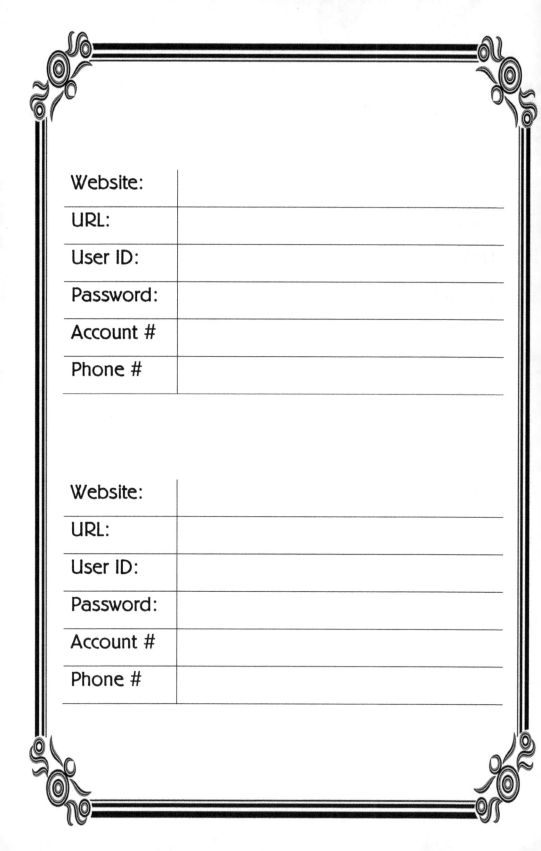

Website:	
URL:	
User ID:	
Password:	
Account #	
Phone #	

Website:	
URL:	
User ID:	
Password:	
Account #	
Phone #	

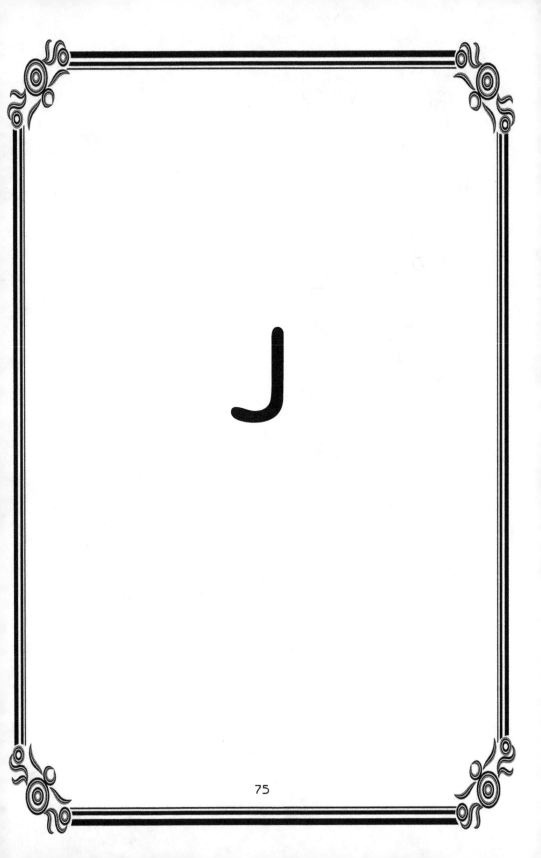

J

Website:	
URL:	
User ID:	
Password:	
Account #	
Phone #	

Website:	
URL:	
User ID:	
Password:	
Account #	
Phone #	

Website:	
URL:	
User ID:	
Password:	
Account #	
Phone #	

Website:	
URL:	
User ID:	
Password:	
Account #	
Phone #	

Website:	
URL:	
User ID:	
Password:	
Account #	
Phone #	

Website:	
URL:	
User ID:	
Password:	
Account #	
Phone #	

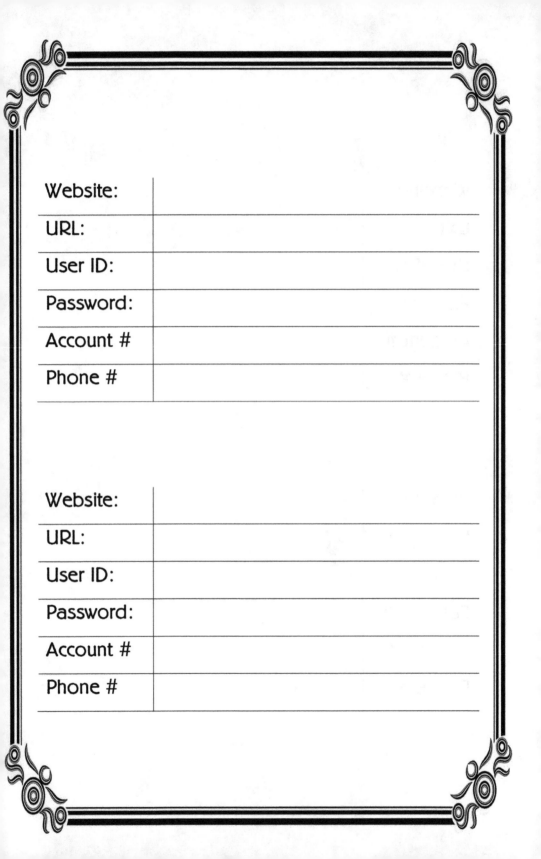

Website:	
URL:	
User ID:	
Password:	
Account #	
Phone #	

Website:	
URL:	
User ID:	
Password:	
Account #	
Phone #	

Website:	
URL:	
User ID:	
Password:	
Account #	
Phone #	

Website:	
URL:	
User ID:	
Password:	
Account #	
Phone #	

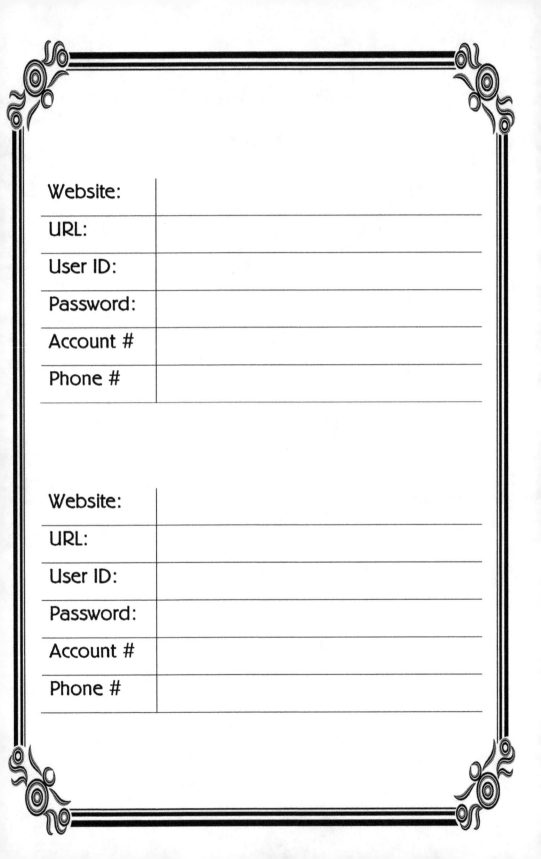

Website:	
URL:	
User ID:	
Password:	
Account #	
Phone #	

Website:	
URL:	
User ID:	
Password:	
Account #	
Phone #	

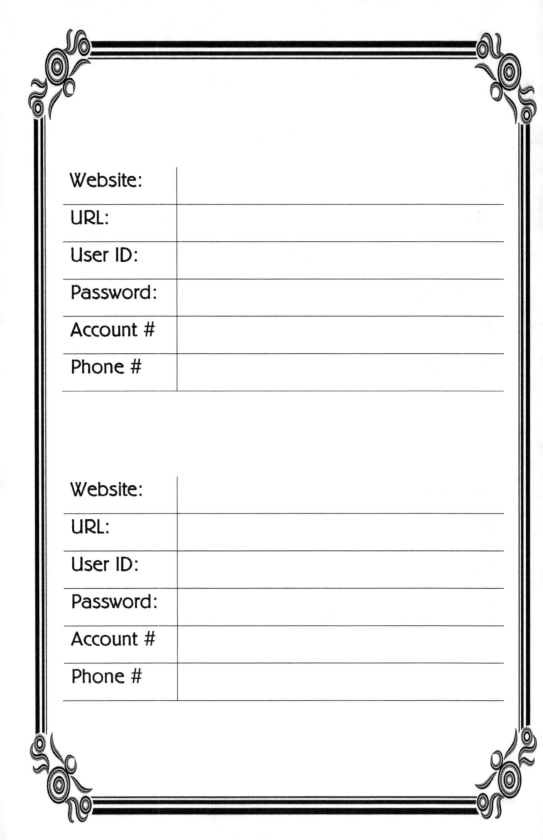

Website:	
URL:	
User ID:	
Password:	
Account #	
Phone #	

Website:	
URL:	
User ID:	
Password:	
Account #	
Phone #	

Website:	
URL:	
User ID:	
Password:	
Account #	
Phone #	

Website:	
URL:	
User ID:	
Password:	
Account #	
Phone #	

Website:	
URL:	
User ID:	
Password:	
Account #	
Phone #	

Website:	
URL:	
User ID:	
Password:	
Account #	
Phone #	

Website:	
URL:	
User ID:	
Password:	
Account #	
Phone #	

Website:	
URL:	
User ID:	
Password:	
Account #	
Phone #	

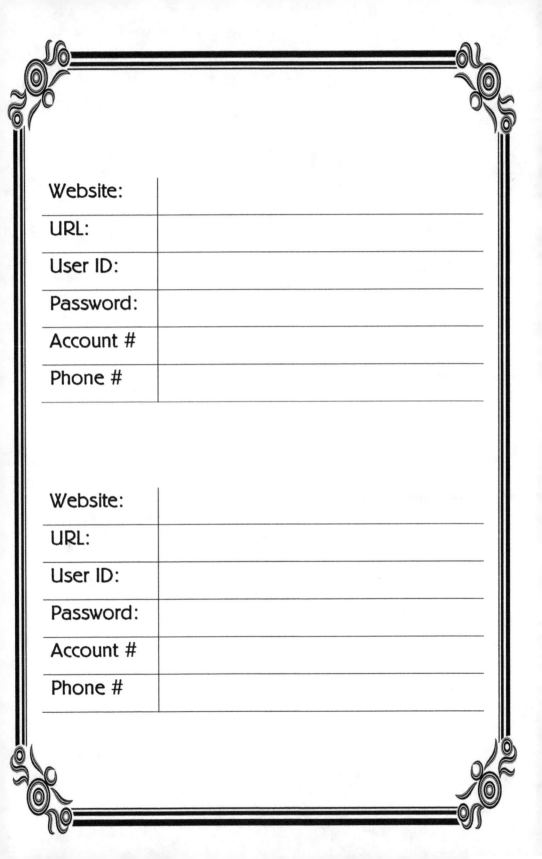

Website:	
URL:	
User ID:	
Password:	
Account #	
Phone #	

Website:	
URL:	
User ID:	
Password:	
Account #	
Phone #	

Website:	
URL:	
User ID:	
Password:	
Account #	
Phone #	

Website:	
URL:	
User ID:	
Password:	
Account #	
Phone #	

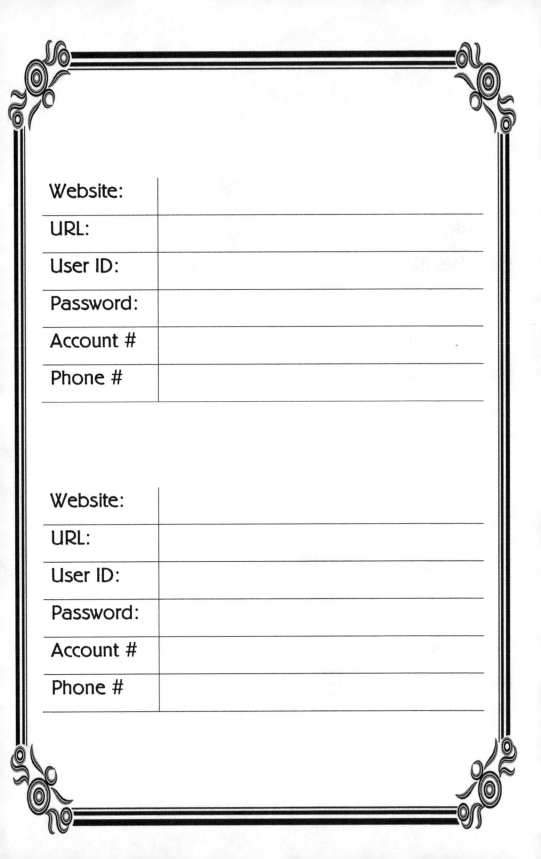

Website:	
URL:	
User ID:	
Password:	
Account #	
Phone #	

Website:	
URL:	
User ID:	
Password:	
Account #	
Phone #	

Website:	
URL:	
User ID:	
Password:	
Account #	
Phone #	

Website:	
URL:	
User ID:	
Password:	
Account #	
Phone #	

L

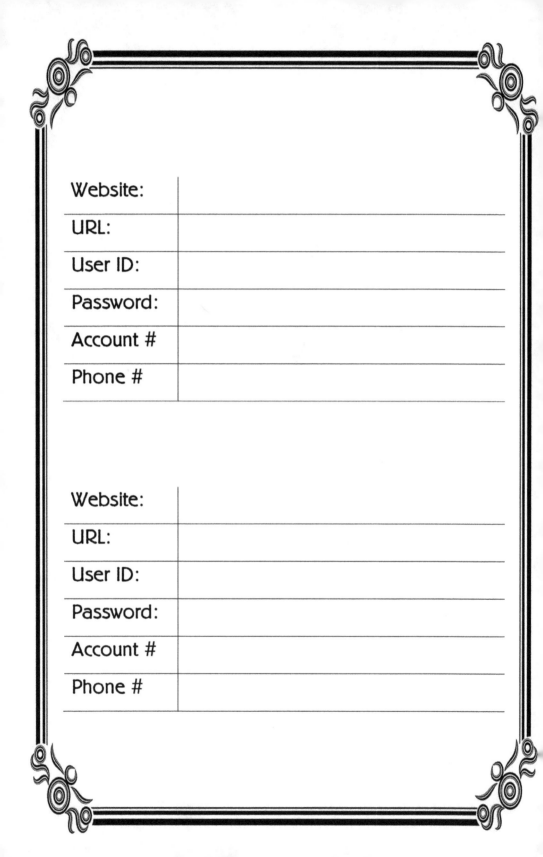

Website:	
URL:	
User ID:	
Password:	
Account #	
Phone #	

Website:	
URL:	
User ID:	
Password:	
Account #	
Phone #	

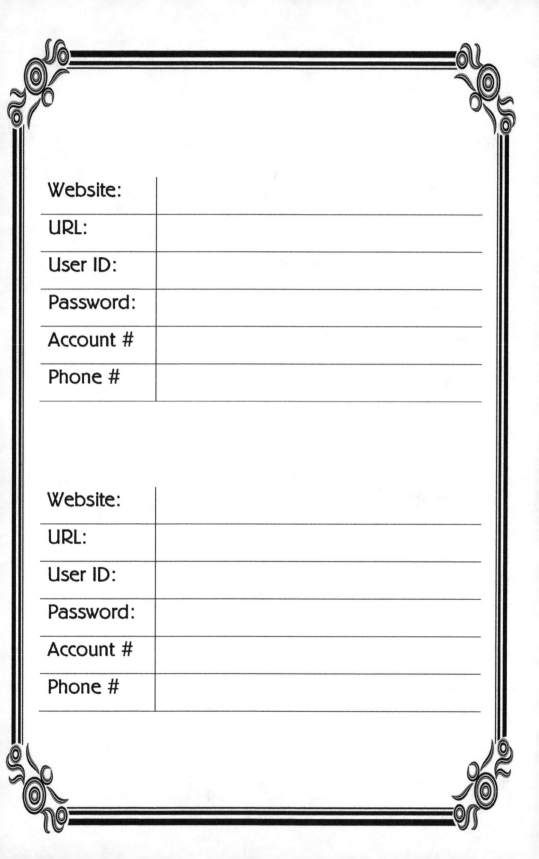

Website:	
URL:	
User ID:	
Password:	
Account #	
Phone #	

Website:	
URL:	
User ID:	
Password:	
Account #	
Phone #	

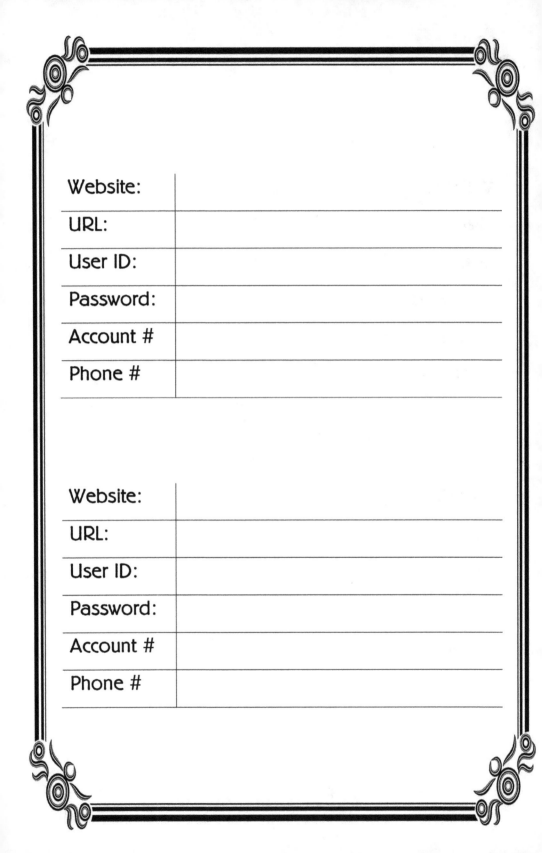

Website:	
URL:	
User ID:	
Password:	
Account #	
Phone #	

Website:	
URL:	
User ID:	
Password:	
Account #	
Phone #	

Website:	
URL:	
User ID:	
Password:	
Account #	
Phone #	

Website:	
URL:	
User ID:	
Password:	
Account #	
Phone #	

Website:	
URL:	
User ID:	
Password:	
Account #	
Phone #	

Website:	
URL:	
User ID:	
Password:	
Account #	
Phone #	

Website:	
URL:	
User ID:	
Password:	
Account #	
Phone #	

Website:	
URL:	
User ID:	
Password:	
Account #	
Phone #	

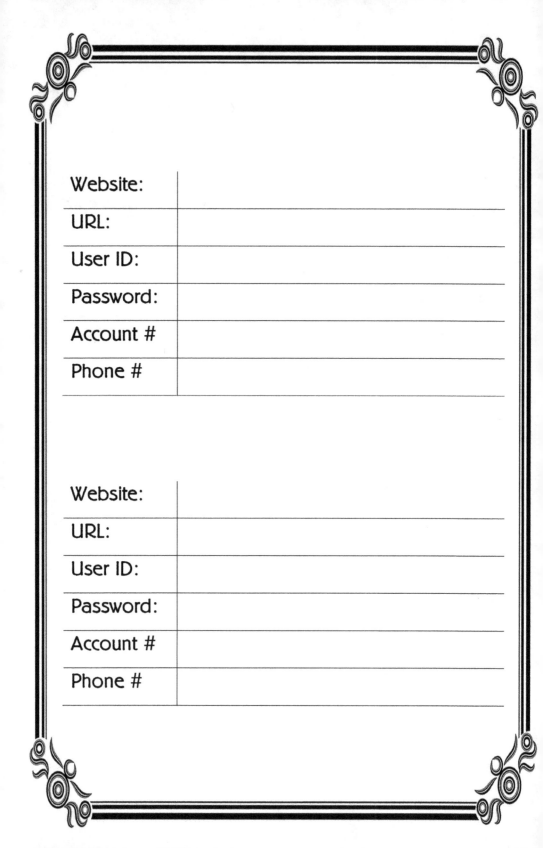

Website:	
URL:	
User ID:	
Password:	
Account #	
Phone #	

Website:	
URL:	
User ID:	
Password:	
Account #	
Phone #	

M

Website:	
URL:	
User ID:	
Password:	
Account #	
Phone #	

Website:	
URL:	
User ID:	
Password:	
Account #	
Phone #	

Website:	
URL:	
User ID:	
Password:	
Account #	
Phone #	

Website:	
URL:	
User ID:	
Password:	
Account #	
Phone #	

Website:	
URL:	
User ID:	
Password:	
Account #	
Phone #	

Website:	
URL:	
User ID:	
Password:	
Account #	
Phone #	

Website:	
URL:	
User ID:	
Password:	
Account #	
Phone #	

Website:	
URL:	
User ID:	
Password:	
Account #	
Phone #	

Website:	
URL:	
User ID:	
Password:	
Account #	
Phone #	

Website:	
URL:	
User ID:	
Password:	
Account #	
Phone #	

Website:	
URL:	
User ID:	
Password:	
Account #	
Phone #	

Website:	
URL:	
User ID:	
Password:	
Account #	
Phone #	

Website:	
URL:	
User ID:	
Password:	
Account #	
Phone #	

Website:	
URL:	
User ID:	
Password:	
Account #	
Phone #	

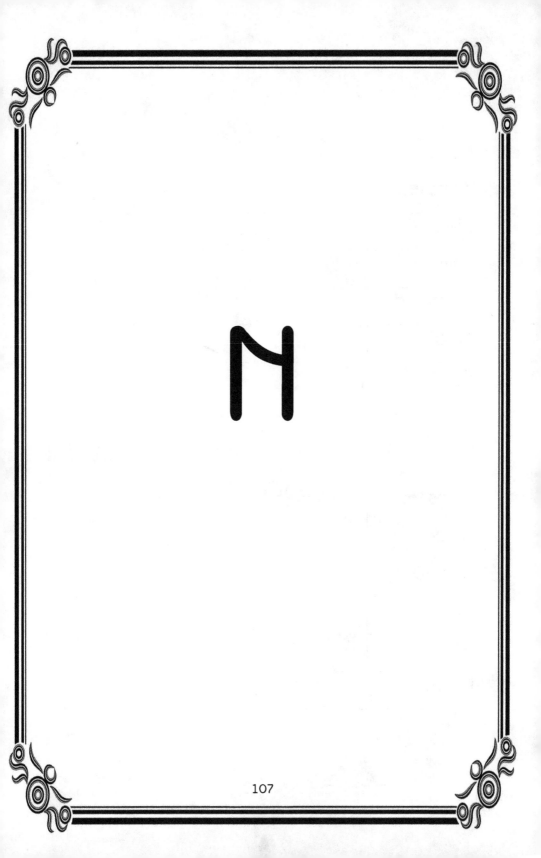

Website:	
URL:	
User ID:	
Password:	
Account #	
Phone #	

Website:	
URL:	
User ID:	
Password:	
Account #	
Phone #	

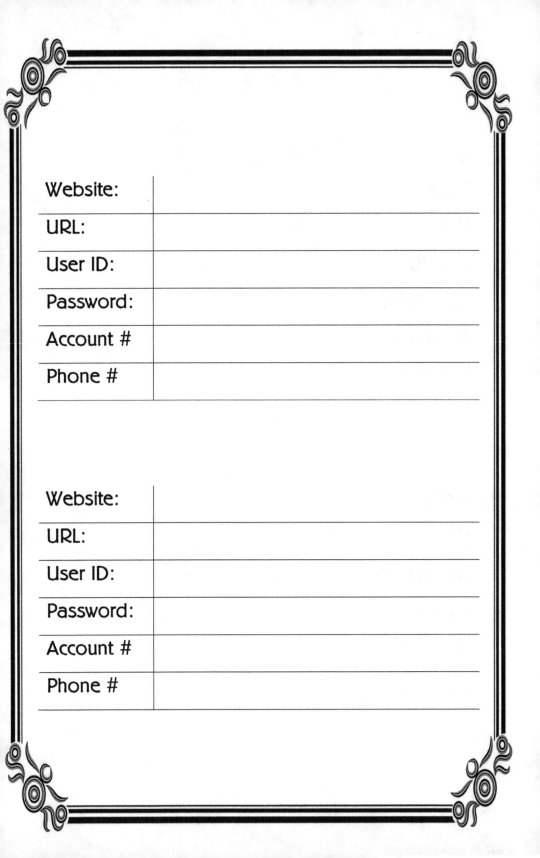

Website:	
URL:	
User ID:	
Password:	
Account #	
Phone #	

Website:	
URL:	
User ID:	
Password:	
Account #	
Phone #	

Website:	
URL:	
User ID:	
Password:	
Account #	
Phone #	

Website:	
URL:	
User ID:	
Password:	
Account #	
Phone #	

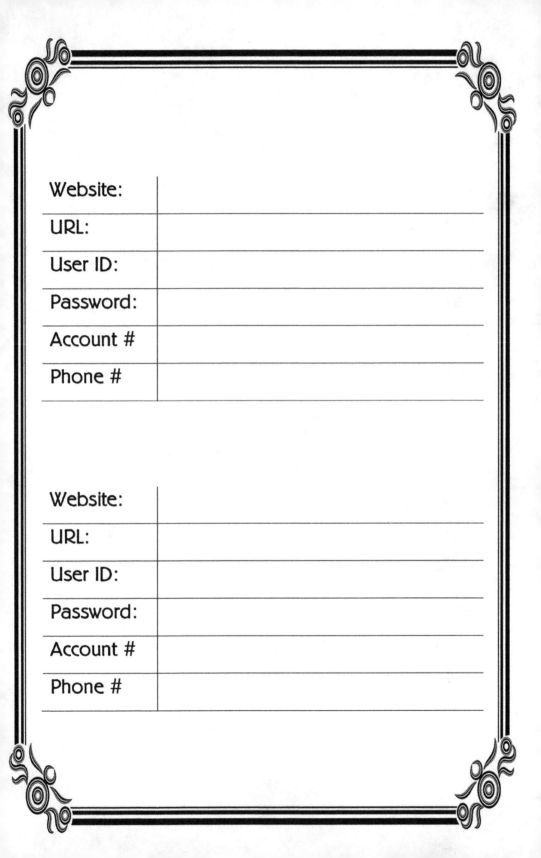

Website:	
URL:	
User ID:	
Password:	
Account #	
Phone #	

Website:	
URL:	
User ID:	
Password:	
Account #	
Phone #	

Website:	
URL:	
User ID:	
Password:	
Account #	
Phone #	

Website:	
URL:	
User ID:	
Password:	
Account #	
Phone #	

Website:	
URL:	
User ID:	
Password:	
Account #	
Phone #	

Website:	
URL:	
User ID:	
Password:	
Account #	
Phone #	

Website:	
URL:	
User ID:	
Password:	
Account #	
Phone #	

Website:	
URL:	
User ID:	
Password:	
Account #	
Phone #	

O

Website:	
URL:	
User ID:	
Password:	
Account #	
Phone #	

Website:	
URL:	
User ID:	
Password:	
Account #	
Phone #	

Website:	
URL:	
User ID:	
Password:	
Account #	
Phone #	

Website:	
URL:	
User ID:	
Password:	
Account #	
Phone #	

Website:	
URL:	
User ID:	
Password:	
Account #	
Phone #	

Website:	
URL:	
User ID:	
Password:	
Account #	
Phone #	

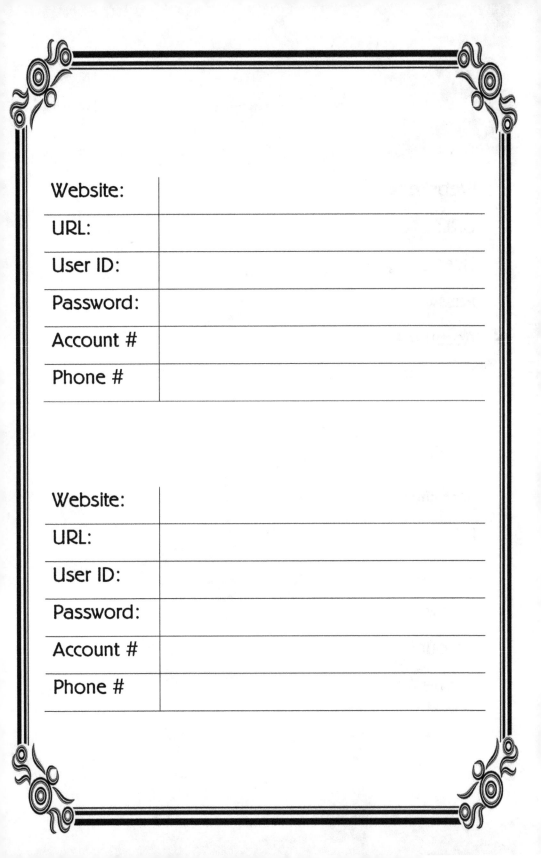

Website:	
URL:	
User ID:	
Password:	
Account #	
Phone #	

Website:	
URL:	
User ID:	
Password:	
Account #	
Phone #	

Website:	
URL:	
User ID:	
Password:	
Account #	
Phone #	

Website:	
URL:	
User ID:	
Password:	
Account #	
Phone #	

P

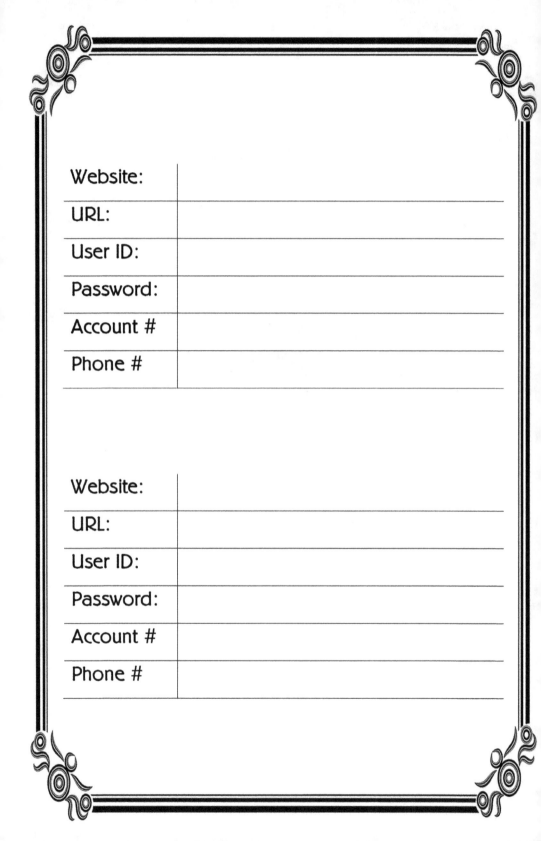

Website:	
URL:	
User ID:	
Password:	
Account #	
Phone #	

Website:	
URL:	
User ID:	
Password:	
Account #	
Phone #	

Website:	
URL:	
User ID:	
Password:	
Account #	
Phone #	

Website:	
URL:	
User ID:	
Password:	
Account #	
Phone #	

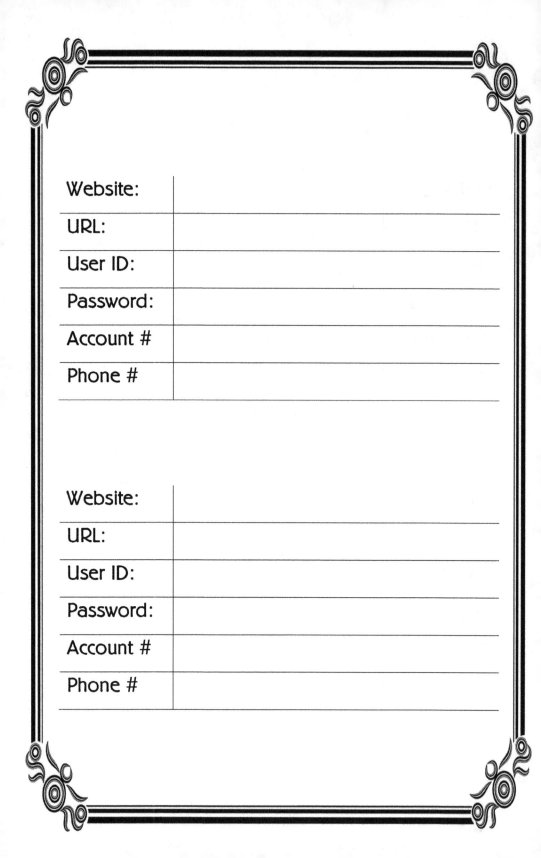

Website:	
URL:	
User ID:	
Password:	
Account #	
Phone #	

Website:	
URL:	
User ID:	
Password:	
Account #	
Phone #	

Website:	
URL:	
User ID:	
Password:	
Account #	
Phone #	

Website:	
URL:	
User ID:	
Password:	
Account #	
Phone #	

Website:	
URL:	
User ID:	
Password:	
Account #	
Phone #	

Website:	
URL:	
User ID:	
Password:	
Account #	
Phone #	

Website:	
URL:	
User ID:	
Password:	
Account #	
Phone #	

Website:	
URL:	
User ID:	
Password:	
Account #	
Phone #	

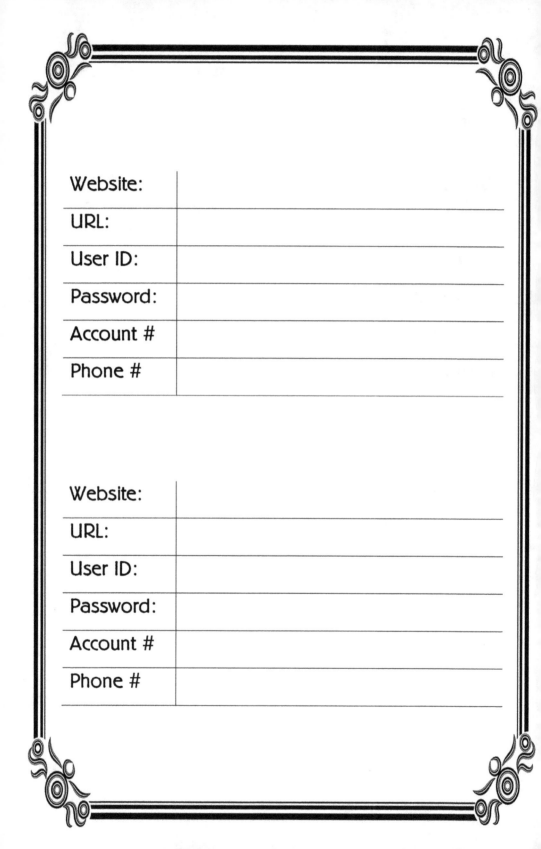

Website:	
URL:	
User ID:	
Password:	
Account #	
Phone #	

Website:	
URL:	
User ID:	
Password:	
Account #	
Phone #	

Website:	
URL:	
User ID:	
Password:	
Account #	
Phone #	

Website:	
URL:	
User ID:	
Password:	
Account #	
Phone #	

Website:	
URL:	
User ID:	
Password:	
Account #	
Phone #	

Website:	
URL:	
User ID:	
Password:	
Account #	
Phone #	

Website:	
URL:	
User ID:	
Password:	
Account #	
Phone #	

Website:	
URL:	
User ID:	
Password:	
Account #	
Phone #	

R

Website:	
URL:	
User ID:	
Password:	
Account #	
Phone #	

Website:	
URL:	
User ID:	
Password:	
Account #	
Phone #	

Website:	
URL:	
User ID:	
Password:	
Account #	
Phone #	

Website:	
URL:	
User ID:	
Password:	
Account #	
Phone #	

Website:	
URL:	
User ID:	
Password:	
Account #	
Phone #	

Website:	
URL:	
User ID:	
Password:	
Account #	
Phone #	

Website:	
URL:	
User ID:	
Password:	
Account #	
Phone #	

Website:	
URL:	
User ID:	
Password:	
Account #	
Phone #	

Website:	
URL:	
User ID:	
Password:	
Account #	
Phone #	

Website:	
URL:	
User ID:	
Password:	
Account #	
Phone #	

Website:	
URL:	
User ID:	
Password:	
Account #	
Phone #	

Website:	
URL:	
User ID:	
Password:	
Account #	
Phone #	

Website:	
URL:	
User ID:	
Password:	
Account #	
Phone #	

Website:	
URL:	
User ID:	
Password:	
Account #	
Phone #	

S

Website:	
URL:	
User ID:	
Password:	
Account #	
Phone #	

Website:	
URL:	
User ID:	
Password:	
Account #	
Phone #	

Website:	
URL:	
User ID:	
Password:	
Account #	
Phone #	

Website:	
URL:	
User ID:	
Password:	
Account #	
Phone #	

Website:	
URL:	
User ID:	
Password:	
Account #	
Phone #	

Website:	
URL:	
User ID:	
Password:	
Account #	
Phone #	

Website:	
URL:	
User ID:	
Password:	
Account #	
Phone #	

Website:	
URL:	
User ID:	
Password:	
Account #	
Phone #	

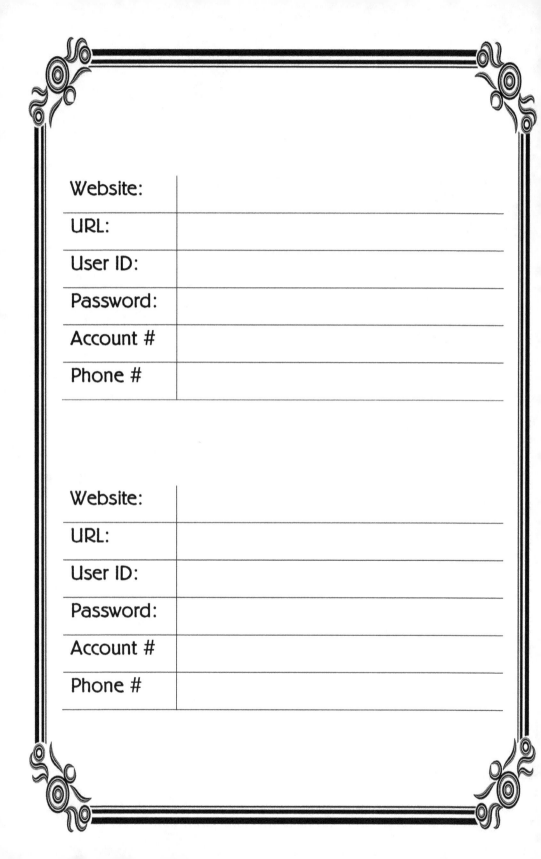

Website:	
URL:	
User ID:	
Password:	
Account #	
Phone #	

Website:	
URL:	
User ID:	
Password:	
Account #	
Phone #	

Website:	
URL:	
User ID:	
Password:	
Account #	
Phone #	

Website:	
URL:	
User ID:	
Password:	
Account #	
Phone #	

Website:	
URL:	
User ID:	
Password:	
Account #	
Phone #	

Website:	
URL:	
User ID:	
Password:	
Account #	
Phone #	

T

Website:	
URL:	
User ID:	
Password:	
Account #	
Phone #	

Website:	
URL:	
User ID:	
Password:	
Account #	
Phone #	

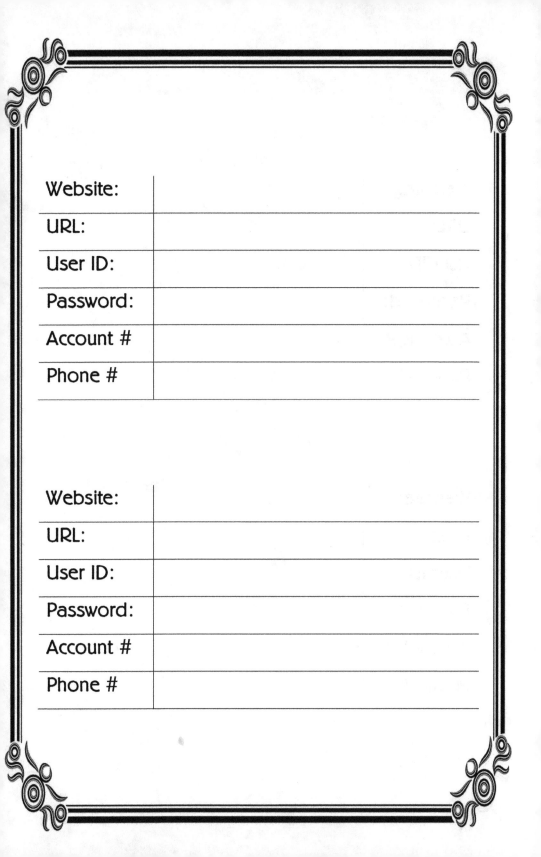

Website:	
URL:	
User ID:	
Password:	
Account #	
Phone #	

Website:	
URL:	
User ID:	
Password:	
Account #	
Phone #	

Website:	
URL:	
User ID:	
Password:	
Account #	
Phone #	

Website:	
URL:	
User ID:	
Password:	
Account #	
Phone #	

Website:	
URL:	
User ID:	
Password:	
Account #	
Phone #	

Website:	
URL:	
User ID:	
Password:	
Account #	
Phone #	

Website:	
URL:	
User ID:	
Password:	
Account #	
Phone #	

Website:	
URL:	
User ID:	
Password:	
Account #	
Phone #	

Website:	
URL:	
User ID:	
Password:	
Account #	
Phone #	

Website:	
URL:	
User ID:	
Password:	
Account #	
Phone #	

Website:	
URL:	
User ID:	
Password:	
Account #	
Phone #	

Website:	
URL:	
User ID:	
Password:	
Account #	
Phone #	

U

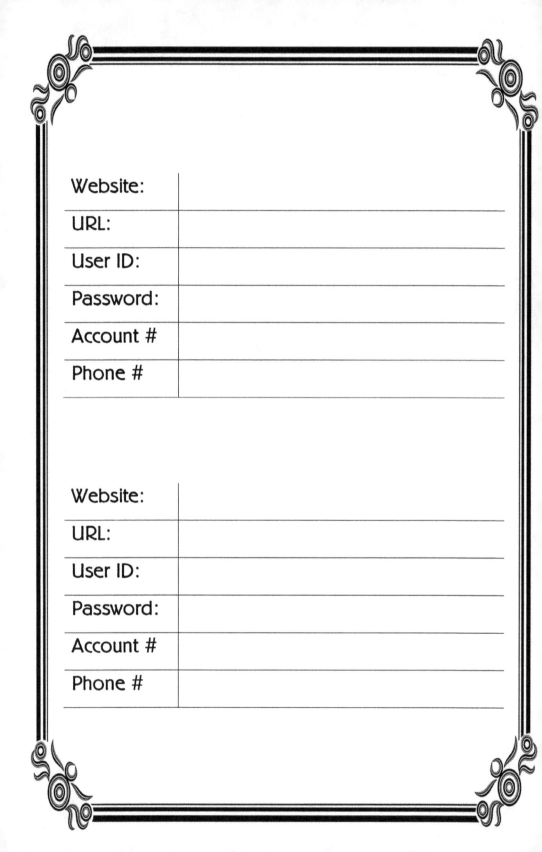

Website:	
URL:	
User ID:	
Password:	
Account #	
Phone #	

Website:	
URL:	
User ID:	
Password:	
Account #	
Phone #	

Website:	
URL:	
User ID:	
Password:	
Account #	
Phone #	

Website:	
URL:	
User ID:	
Password:	
Account #	
Phone #	

Website:	
URL:	
User ID:	
Password:	
Account #	
Phone #	

Website:	
URL:	
User ID:	
Password:	
Account #	
Phone #	

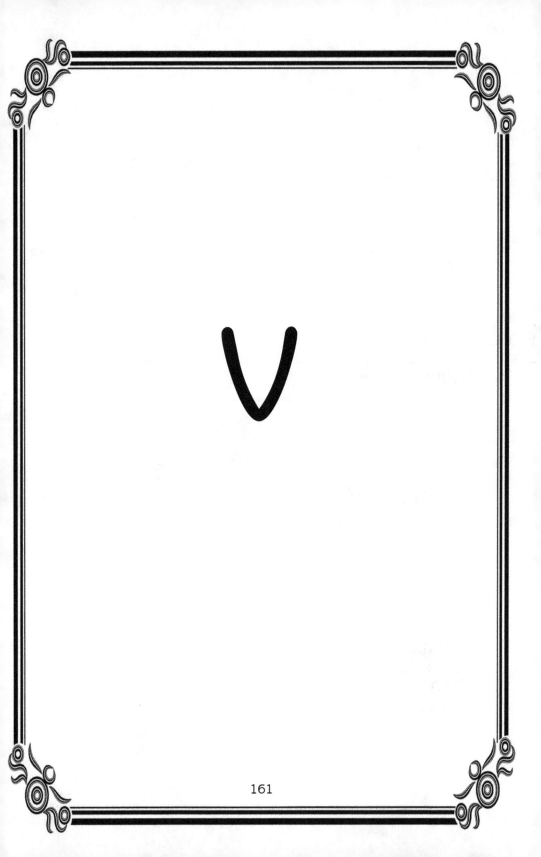

Website:	
URL:	
User ID:	
Password:	
Account #	
Phone #	

Website:	
URL:	
User ID:	
Password:	
Account #	
Phone #	

Website:	
URL:	
User ID:	
Password:	
Account #	
Phone #	

Website:	
URL:	
User ID:	
Password:	
Account #	
Phone #	

Website:	
URL:	
User ID:	
Password:	
Account #	
Phone #	

Website:	
URL:	
User ID:	
Password:	
Account #	
Phone #	

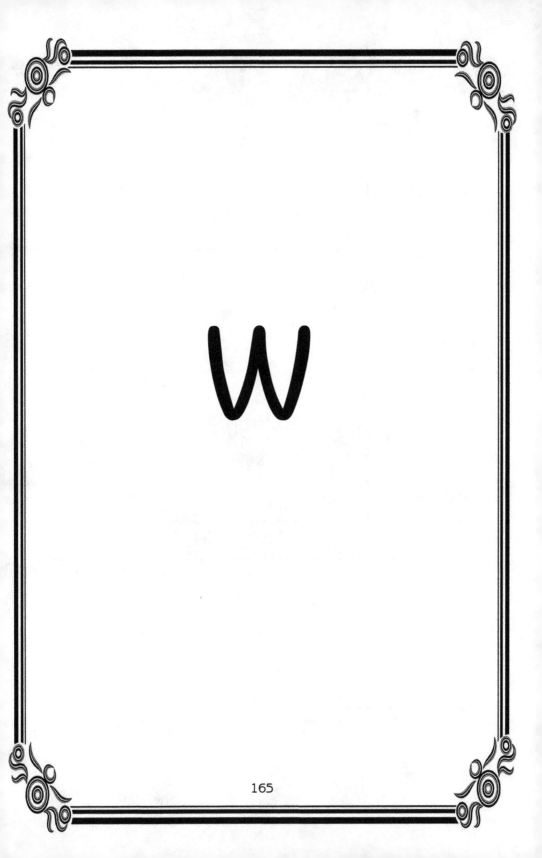

Website:	
URL:	
User ID:	
Password:	
Account #	
Phone #	

Website:	
URL:	
User ID:	
Password:	
Account #	
Phone #	

Website:	
URL:	
User ID:	
Password:	
Account #	
Phone #	

Website:	
URL:	
User ID:	
Password:	
Account #	
Phone #	

Website:	
URL:	
User ID:	
Password:	
Account #	
Phone #	

Website:	
URL:	
User ID:	
Password:	
Account #	
Phone #	

Website:	
URL:	
User ID:	
Password:	
Account #	
Phone #	

Website:	
URL:	
User ID:	
Password:	
Account #	
Phone #	

Website:	
URL:	
User ID:	
Password:	
Account #	
Phone #	

Website:	
URL:	
User ID:	
Password:	
Account #	
Phone #	

Website:	
URL:	
User ID:	
Password:	
Account #	
Phone #	

Website:	
URL:	
User ID:	
Password:	
Account #	
Phone #	

Website:	
URL:	
User ID:	
Password:	
Account #	
Phone #	

Website:	
URL:	
User ID:	
Password:	
Account #	
Phone #	

XYZ

Website:	
URL:	
User ID:	
Password:	
Account #	
Phone #	

Website:	
URL:	
User ID:	
Password:	
Account #	
Phone #	

Website:	
URL:	
User ID:	
Password:	
Account #	
Phone #	

Website:	
URL:	
User ID:	
Password:	
Account #	
Phone #	

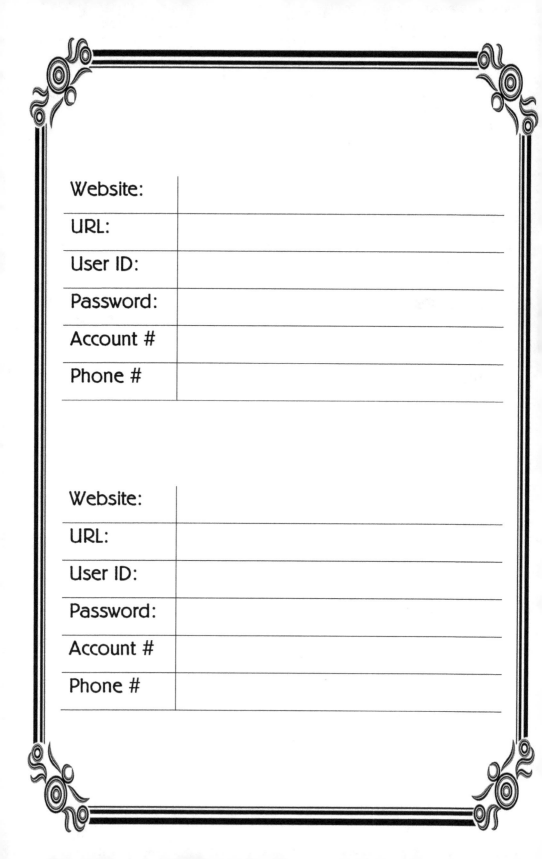

Website:	
URL:	
User ID:	
Password:	
Account #	
Phone #	

Website:	
URL:	
User ID:	
Password:	
Account #	
Phone #	

Website:	
URL:	
User ID:	
Password:	
Account #	
Phone #	

Website:	
URL:	
User ID:	
Password:	
Account #	
Phone #	

Website:	
URL:	
User ID:	
Password:	
Account #	
Phone #	

Website:	
URL:	
User ID:	
Password:	
Account #	
Phone #	

Website:	
URL:	
User ID:	
Password:	
Account #	
Phone #	

Website:	
URL:	
User ID:	
Password:	
Account #	
Phone #	

Website:	
URL:	
User ID:	
Password:	
Account #	
Phone #	

Website:	
URL:	
User ID:	
Password:	
Account #	
Phone #	

Website:	
URL:	
User ID:	
Password:	
Account #	
Phone #	

Website:	
URL:	
User ID:	
Password:	
Account #	
Phone #	

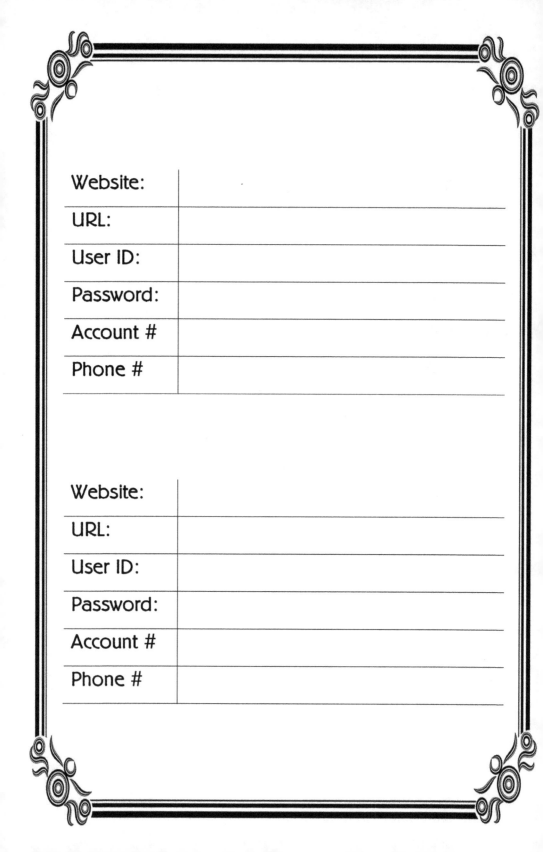

Website:	
URL:	
User ID:	
Password:	
Account #	
Phone #	

Website:	
URL:	
User ID:	
Password:	
Account #	
Phone #	

SECURITY QUESTIONS

What is your mother's maiden name?

_____

What street did you live on in first grade?

_____

Who is your favorite author?

_____

What is the make / model of your first car?

_____

Where was your first kiss?

_____

What was your high school mascot?

_____

What's your spouse's middle name?

_____

What was the name of your first pet?

_____

What is your oldest sibling's first name?

_____

What is your paternal grandfather's middle name?

_____

Where did you get married?

_____

Where were your parents married?

_____

Where did your parents meet?

_____

What is your favorite color?

_____

What is your oldest child's first name?

_____

What is your youngest sibling's first name?

_____

What color is your vehicle?

_____

What is your favorite grocery store?

_____

What is your youngest child's name?

_____

What is your grandmother's maiden name?

_____

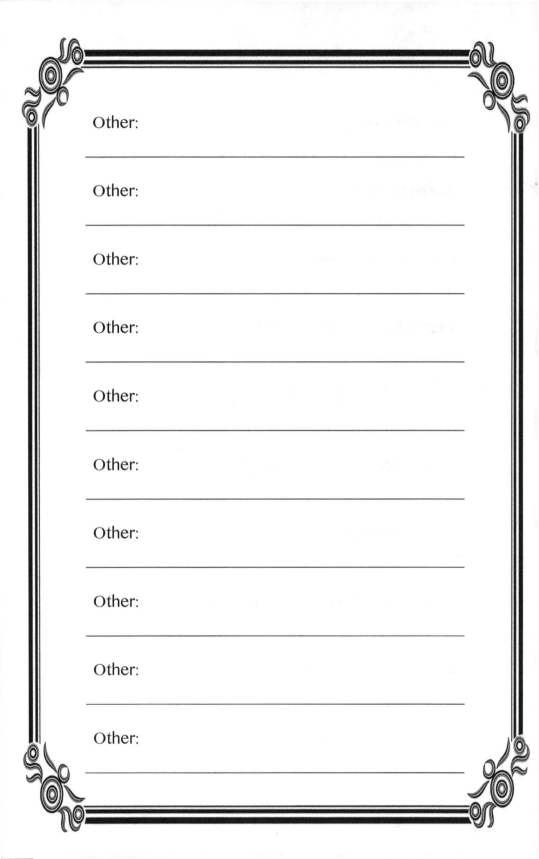

Other:

_____

Other:

_____

Other:

_____

Other:

_____

Other:

_____

Other:

_____

Other:

_____

Other:

_____

Other:

_____

Other:

_____